Sto

FRIENDS
OF ACPL

WINGS, LEGS, OR FINS

Wings, Legs, or Fins

By HENRY B. KANE

Alfred A. Knopf New York

For Elizabeth Kane Chaffee, who came from there to here

L.C. Catalog card number: 63–14608

THIS IS A BORZOI BOOK, PUBLISHED BY ALFRED A. KNOPF, INC.

All life began in the water. That was long, long ago. Today, many creatures still make their homes there. But others have come ashore to live. They move about on the surface of the land, or burrow beneath it. And many have taken to the air.

Lie on your stomach on the grass in summer. Watch a caterpillar humping along. It reaches out to pull itself from one blade to another. Over there, a tiny ant pulls a dead insect three times its size through the grass jungle. Roll over and watch a bird flying high across the sky. At the edge of nearby woods, a squirrel races up the trunk of a tree.

Fish swim. Grasshoppers leap. Snakes crawl. Birds fly. Men walk. The creatures of the world have found ways of moving about—of getting from here to there.

SWIMMING

Many kinds of creatures move on or through the waters of the world. There are fish in great numbers. The little sunfish or pumpkin-seed swims in the same way that most fishes do. It sweeps its tail fin from side to side to push forward.

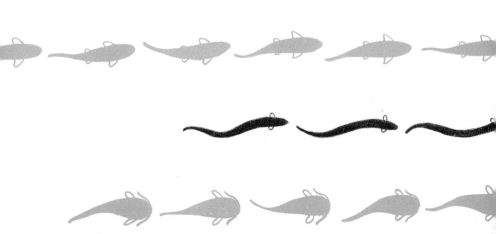

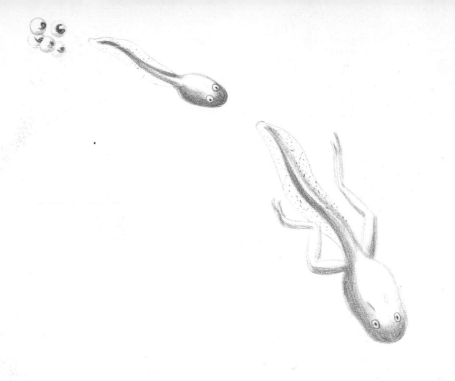

The frog is an amphibian. It hatches from an egg laid in the water, and spends the first part of its life as a tadpole. It breathes by means of gills like a fish. Then, it grows legs, breathes air directly, and its tail shrinks away. The frog swims by kicking its big, webbed feet out behind, pushing against the water.

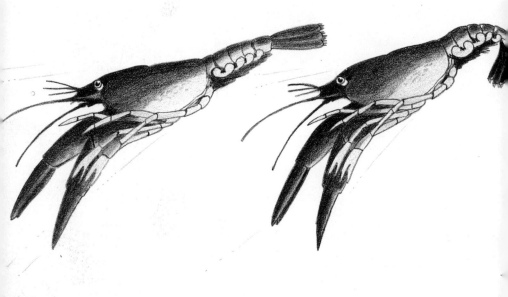

The crayfish is a small, fresh-water cousin of the lobster. It walks along the bottom of ponds and streams. When a crayfish is in a hurry, though, it does not walk. It slaps its big, flat tail against its underside. This shoots it backward through the water at an amazing speed.

Most turtles make their home in the water. They can stay underwater for a long time. But they must come to the surface to breathe. A turtle uses its feet like oars, but not together in pairs, as in rowing a boat. Each foot pushes back against the water at a different time.

Among the biggest water birds is the Canada goose. It has webbed feet which paddle it gracefully across the surface of the water. It cannot dive, but often tips up in shallow water to reach for food on the bottom.

The muskrat is a close relative of many of our native mice and rats. It is more at home in the water than on land. A muskrat dives to the bottom of a pond to pull up a juicy plant stem. He returns to the surface to eat it, then dives back again for another.

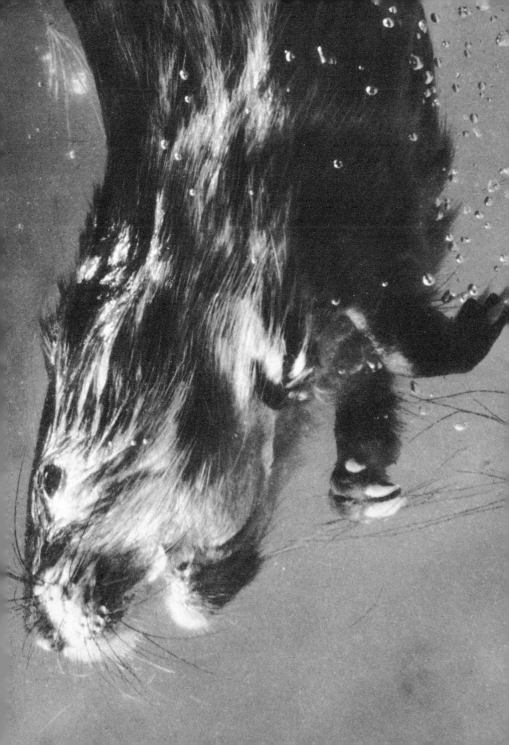

CRAWLING

Some creatures move by crawling. Not all of them do it in the same way, or at the same speed. A snail glides along slowly with a wavelike movement. Its one broad foot lays a trail of slime to make a smooth path.

Many millions of years ago, the ancestors of snakes had legs. Through the years, the legs have disappeared. Now the snake crawls on its belly in a series of S-shaped movements. From the speed with which some snakes move, their lost legs are not missed.

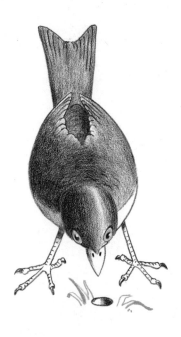

An earthworm's body is made up of many segments. It crawls by stretching some of these segments forward. Then it shortens them to pull other segments ahead. It is somewhat like an elastic band that is being stretched and released.

LEAPING

Most creatures can jump or leap to some extent. There are some that do this much better than others. Like rabbits, they are usually animals whose hind legs are longer than their front legs.

The katydid is a long-horned grasshopper. The *katydid, katydidn't* song of the male is made when it rubs its wing covers together. The katydid hears through its front legs. It has very long hind legs which shoot it into the air. Then the wings take over to extend the leap.

When a frog is going a short distance, it hops. When it is startled, it makes long leaps. That is where the game of leapfrog gets its name. During the jump, the frog's third eyelid closes to protect the eye from damage.

Some fish, like this trout, leap from the water. Usually, it is to catch insects on or above the surface. But there are fish that seem to do it just for fun.

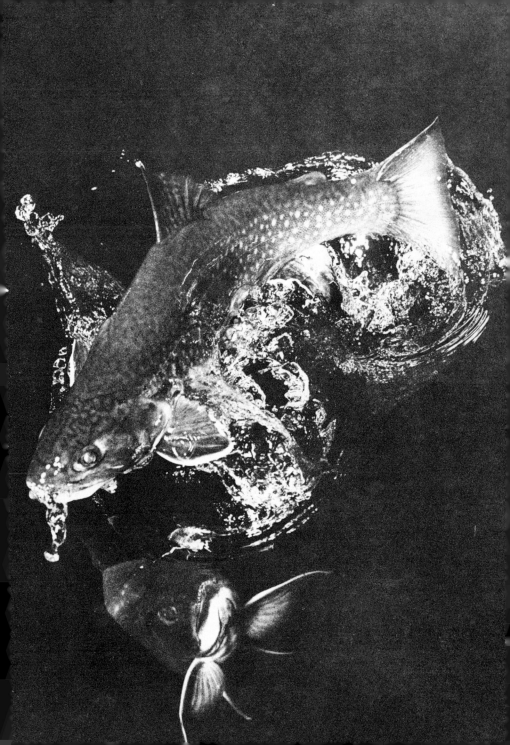

There are mice that walk and run, others that leap. The white-footed mouse does all three, and also climbs trees and bushes with ease. It sleeps during the day and wakes up at dusk.

The wood duck nests in trees. When the ducklings are less than a day old, their mother calls to them from outside the nest hole. One by one, they clamber to the edge of the hole and leap off into space. Their little wings flap wildly to hold them right side up.

All squirrels leap from tree to tree.
When a flying squirrel does so, it
spreads its legs wide. This stretches
the loose skin between them. Then,
like a furry flying carpet, it glides to
the trunk of another tree.

WALKING

Man walks on two legs. Other creatures walk on four, six, or even more legs. A caterpillar, with several legs, leaves tracks something like a tiny tractor.

An inchworm is a caterpillar with legs only at the front and rear. It walks in loops. First it stretches its body forward as far as possible. Then it brings its hind legs up to its front legs. In this way, it inches along a twig.

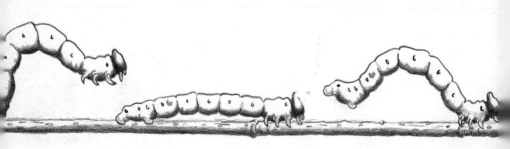

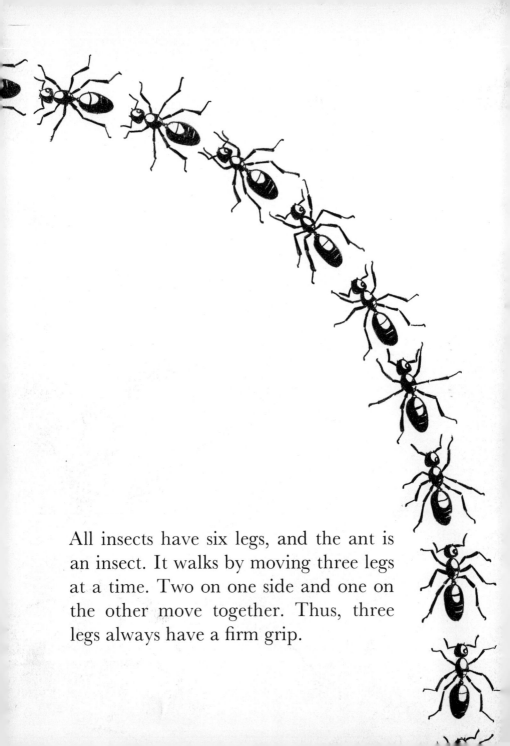

All insects have six legs, and the ant is an insect. It walks by moving three legs at a time. Two on one side and one on the other move together. Thus, three legs always have a firm grip.

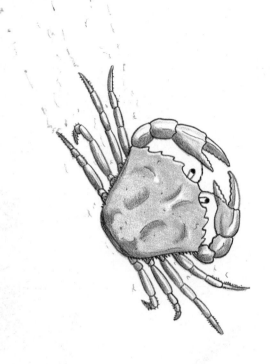

The crab lives in salt water, usually along the shore. It scuttles away sideways when it is disturbed. Its big pincer claws are held up for protection.

When the day-old wood duckling lands on the ground, it waits there patiently. At last, all its brothers and sisters have joined it. Then they follow their mother off to the nearest bit of water.

The crow is an intelligent bird. It is as much at home on the ground as in the air. It struts along, hunting for grasshoppers and other insects in the grass with other crows. And, always, there is a lookout, ready to give the alarm in case of danger.

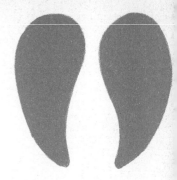

A walking deer moves a front leg and the rear leg on the other side at the same time. All four-legged animals walk this way. It helps them keep their balance. But, when a deer is in a hurry, it bounds through the woods. Then both legs hind work together like steel springs.

FLYING

After creatures emerged from the sea, they learned to crawl. Then they learned to walk and leap. And, at last, some learned to fly. They had freed themselves from an earth-bound life. Many and varied are those that have taken to the air.

The white-faced hornet builds gray, paper nests in trees and under the eaves of houses. When it flies, its two pairs of wings beat up and down. On the down stroke, the flat of the wing pushes against the air. Then it twists to cut down air resistance on the up stroke.

The only mammal that can really fly is the bat. Most bats are small, mouselike creatures with long, thin fingers. A thin skin spreads between the fingers, forming a wing. The skin also extends down to the tail. The bat sleeps all day. It comes out at dusk to hunt insects through the darkening sky.

Of all the flyers, the bird is the best known. Its wings, like those of the bat, have arms, wrists, and hands. These are hidden from view by the wings' feather coverings.

The petrel is a long-winged bird no bigger than a robin. Except during the nesting season, it spends all its life at sea. It skims and flutters just above the waves. Sometimes it bobs about on the surface, riding out even the worst storms.

Most owls sleep during the day. After dark, the owl's big, sharp eyes and keen ears locate unsuspecting mice and rabbits. Then, on silent wings, it swoops down to strike. Owls are hunters of the night.

So, now you know how birds, and beasts, and some other creatures get from here to there.